BULLS
23

D1241206

LANEY
23

USA
9

NORTH
23
CAROLINA

Little People, BIG DREAMS™

MICHAEL JORDAN

Written by
Maria Isabel Sánchez Vegara

Illustrated by
Lo Harris

Frances Lincoln
Children's Books

Little Michael grew up in a town in North Carolina. He was the fourth kid of the Jordans, but he always wanted to be the first at everything. Especially if that meant beating his older brother, Larry.

Hoping they would not just be fierce competitors but good teammates, his parents encouraged their kids to play all kinds of sports. And Michael learned that talent may win a game, but only teamwork can win a championship.

One day, Michael came home from school crying. He hadn't been selected for the basketball team because he was too short! His mother wiped his tears and told him what she used to say to all her kids: "Go out and earn it."

Michael spent all summer practicing with the ball. When it was time to go back to class, he had not just gained self-confidence; he had grown taller, too. Soon, he was the star of the Buccaneers, his high school team.

Whether it was defending the hoop, stealing balls, or making impossible jumps, he was the best on the court. Many colleges set their sights on him, and Michael accepted a scholarship to the University of North Carolina.

Michael went from scoring the winning shot at the college finals to receiving a gold medal at the Olympics. With "23" on his back, he joined the Chicago Bulls at the NBA, the biggest professional league in the world.

The Bulls had never landed a title. Still, Michael was there to do what teammates do: help each other become better players. Six years later, they won their first championship and they kept winning—three times in a row!

When the best NBA stars were invited to participate at the Olympics, Michael knew that the gold medal would come home with them. The whole world went wild watching the Dream Team, the most incredible team ever assembled.

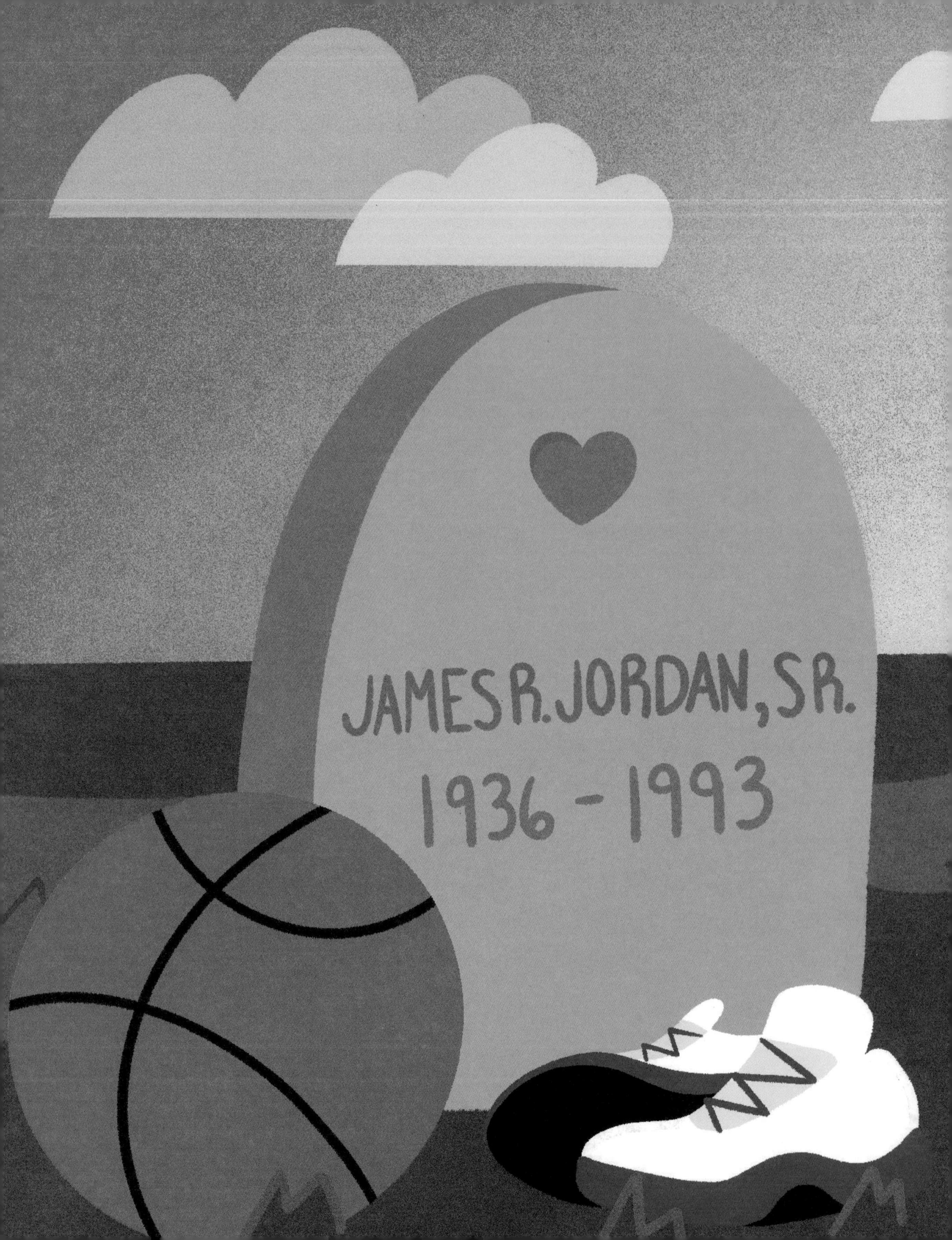
JAMES R. JORDAN, SR.
1936 - 1993

Michael was so famous that even a pair of sneakers were named after him! But when his father died, he was heartbroken and quit basketball. He sought comfort playing baseball, his dad's favorite sport.

It took him a year to realize that his place was on the basketball court, next to his teammates. Everyone who loved the game was happy to see Michael lead the Bulls to win their fourth championship on a very special date: Father's Day.

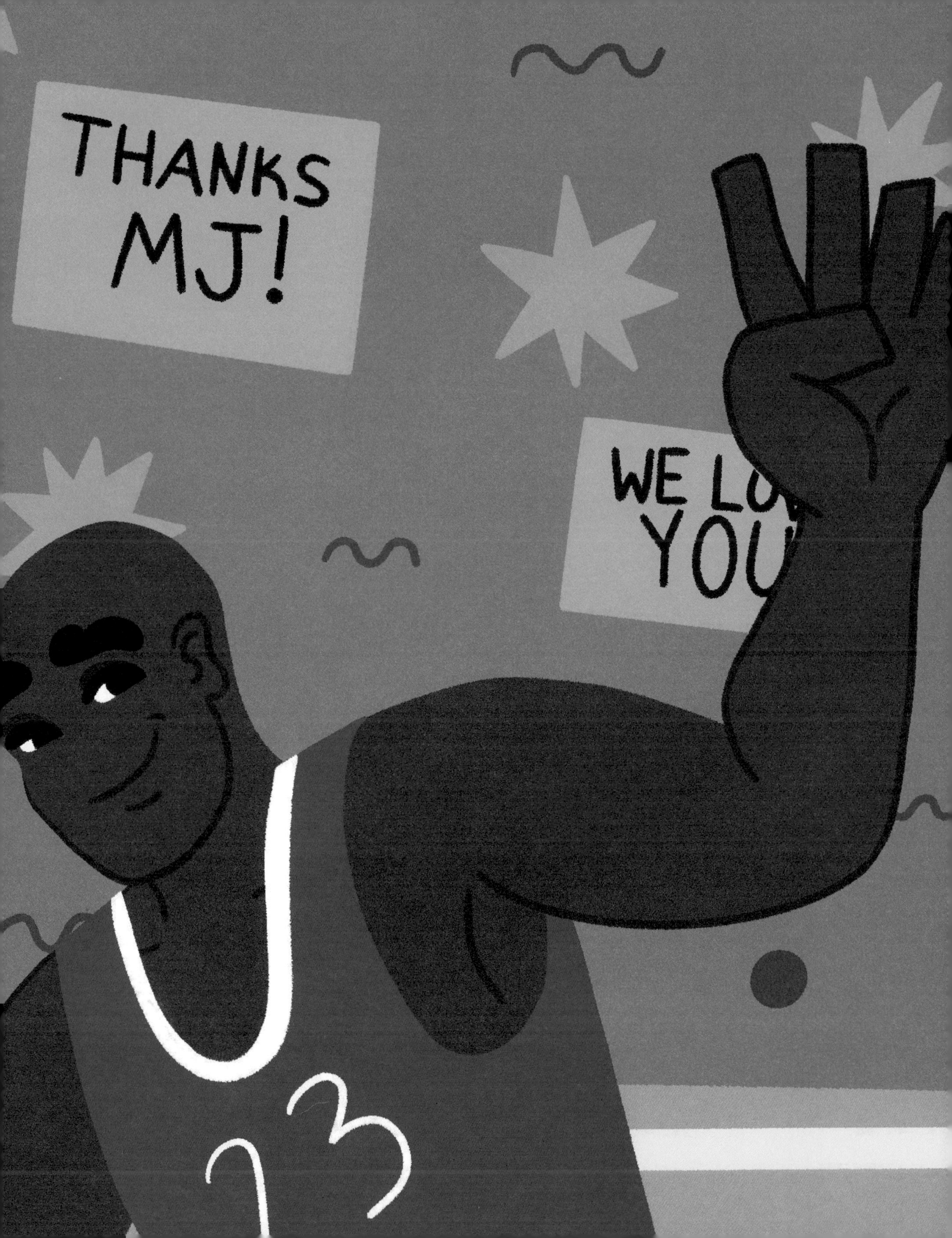
THANKS MJ!
WE LO
YOU
23

One day, his coach Phil announced that it was his last season with the team. Michael and his teammates wanted to make sure it ended right! And after winning his sixth title, it was time for His Airness to hang up his sneakers, too.

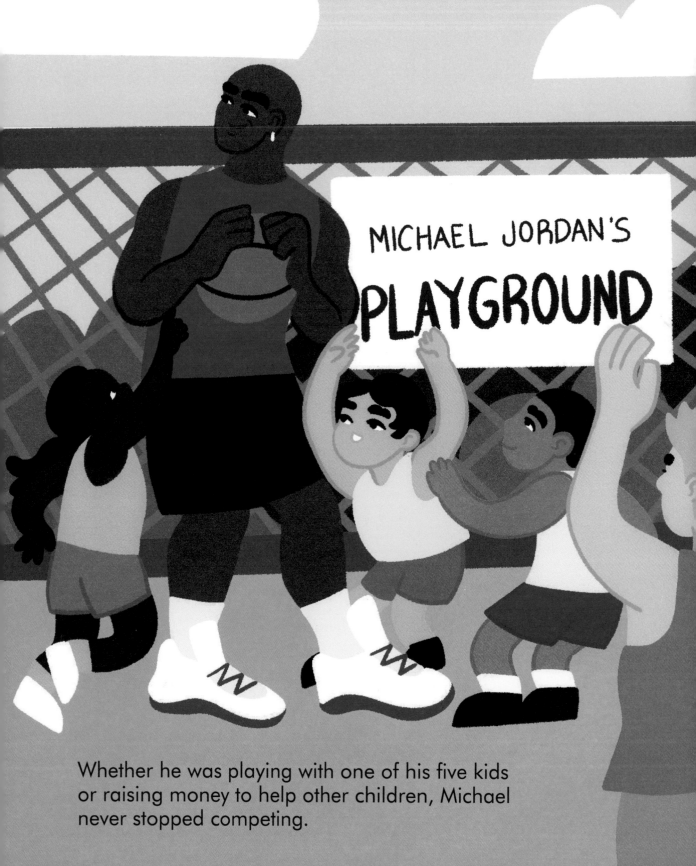

Whether he was playing with one of his five kids or raising money to help other children, Michael never stopped competing.

He became a successful businessman supporting
all kinds of sports: from golf to car racing.

By expecting things of himself before he could even
do them, little Michael became the biggest legend in
the history of basketball. And an inspiration for others
to choose their dream… and make it happen!

MICHAEL JORDAN

(Born 1963)

c. 1979   1980

Michael Jordan was born on February 17th, 1963, in Brooklyn, New York. One of five children, Michael's family moved to Wilmington, North Carolina, when he was very young. His father was a General Electric plant supervisor, and his mother worked at a bank. Michael loved sports, and his parents encouraged him to try everything. He didn't make his high school basketball team as a sophomore... but he trained hard and the following year, he made the team! After high school, he won a basketball scholarship to the University of North Carolina, where he played under head coach Dean Smith. In Michael's first season at North Carolina he was named Rookie of the Year for 1982. He was selected by the Chicago Bulls of the National Basketball Association (NBA) as the third pick of the

1995

2014

1984 draft. He went on to play 1,072 NBA games, becoming known for his "airtime"—a 4-foot vertical leap for the basket—taking the Bulls to six NBA championships with his coach, Phil Jackson. He won Most Valuable Player four times, as well as two Olympic Gold medals as part of America's most famous national squad: the Dream Team. When he retired from basketball, his determination never left him, believing that "you have to expect things of yourself before you can do them." He has gone on to run charities, make movies, and work in business. In 2016, he was presented with the Presidential Medal of Freedom by Barack Obama. Today, Michael is loved by people all over the world, and is considered by basketball fans as the greatest player to ever step onto the court.

Want to find out more about Michael Jordan?

Have a read of this great book:

Salt in his Shoes by Deloris Jordan

Brimming with creative inspiration, how-to projects, and useful information to enrich your everyday life, Quarto Knows is a favourite destination for those pursuing their interests and passions. Visit our site and dig deeper with our books into your area of interest: Quarto Creates, Quarto Cooks, Quarto Homes, Quarto Lives, Quarto Drives, Quarto Explores, Quarto Gifts, or Quarto Kids.

Text © 2021 Maria Isabel Sánchez Vegara. Illustrations © 2021 Lo Harris.
Original concept of the series by Maria Isabel Sánchez Vegara, published by Alba Editorial, s.l.u
Little People Big Dreams and Pequeña&Grande are registered trademarks of Alba Editorial, s.l.u. for books, printed publications, e-books and audiobooks. Produced under licence from Alba Editorial, s.l.u.
First Published in the USA in 2021 by Frances Lincoln Children's Books, an imprint of The Quarto Group.
Quarto Boston North Shore, 100 Cummings Center, Suite 265D, Beverly, MA 01915, USA
Tel: +1 978-282-9590, Fax: +1 978-283-2742 **www.QuartoKnows.com**
All rights reserved.

A catalogue record for this book is available from the British Library.
ISBN 978-0-7112-5938-6
Set in Futura BT.

Published by Katie Cotton • Designed by Karissa Santos • Edited by Katy Flint and Rachel Williams
Production by Nikki Ingram • Editorial Assistance from Alex Hithersay and Rachel Robinson
Manufactured in Guangdong, China CC082021
1 3 5 7 9 8 6 4 2

Photographic acknowledgements (pages 28-29, from left to right): 1. DATE UNKNOWN; Wilmington, NC, USA; Michael Jordan little league photo from the late 1970s © Wilmington StarNews – USA TODAY NETWORK. 2. University of North Carolina's Michael Jordan #23 eyes the basket before shooting from the foul line during a game © Focus on Sport via Getty Images. 3. Michael Jordan of the Chicago Bulls cuts through traffic to dunk the ball in the third quarter 20 April against the Detroit Pistons at the United Center in Chicago © BRIAN BAHR/AFP via Getty Images. 4. Charlotte Hornets owner Michael Jordan looks on during a game against the Atlanta Hawks at the Time Warner Cable Arena on November 1, 2015 in Charlotte, North Carolina © Chris Elise/NBAE via Getty Images

Collect the *Little People*, **BIG DREAMS**™ series:

FRIDA KAHLO	**COCO CHANEL**	**MAYA ANGELOU**	**AMELIA EARHART**	**AGATHA CHRISTIE**	**MARIE CURIE**	**ROSA PARKS**

AUDREY HEPBURN	**EMMELINE PANKHURST**	**ELLA FITZGERALD**	**ADA LOVELACE**	**JANE AUSTEN**	**GEORGIA O'KEEFFE**	**HARRIET TUBMAN**

ANNE FRANK	**MOTHER TERESA**	**JOSEPHINE BAKER**	**L. M. MONTGOMERY**	**JANE GOODALL**	**SIMONE DE BEAUVOIR**	**MUHAMMAD ALI**

STEPHEN HAWKING	**MARIA MONTESSORI**	**VIVIENNE WESTWOOD**	**MAHATMA GANDHI**	**DAVID BOWIE**	**WILMA RUDOLPH**	**DOLLY PARTON**

BRUCE LEE	**RUDOLF NUREYEV**	**ZAHA HADID**	**MARY SHELLEY**	**MARTIN LUTHER KING JR.**	**DAVID ATTENBOROUGH**	**ASTRID LINDGREN**

EVONNE GOOLAGONG	**BOB DYLAN**	**ALAN TURING**	**BILLIE JEAN KING**	**GRETA THUNBERG**	**JESSE OWENS**	**JEAN-MICHEL BASQUIAT**

ARETHA FRANKLIN

CORAZON AQUINO

PELÉ

ERNEST SHACKLETON

STEVE JOBS

AYRTON SENNA

LOUISE BOURGEOIS

ELTON JOHN

JOHN LENNON

PRINCE

CHARLES DARWIN

CAPTAIN TOM MOORE

HANS CHRISTIAN ANDERSEN

STEVIE WONDER

MEGAN RAPINOE

MARY ANNING

MALALA YOUSAFZAI

ANDY WARHOL

RUPAUL

MICHELLE OBAMA

MINDY KALING

IRIS APFEL

ROSALIND FRANKLIN

RUTH BADER GINSBURG

MARILYN MONROE

KAMALA HARRIS

ALBERT EINSTEIN

CHARLES DICKENS

YOKO ONO

ACTIVITY BOOKS

STICKER ACTIVITY BOOK

COLORING BOOK

LITTLE ME, BIG DREAMS JOURNAL

Discover more about the series at www.littlepeoplebigdreams.com

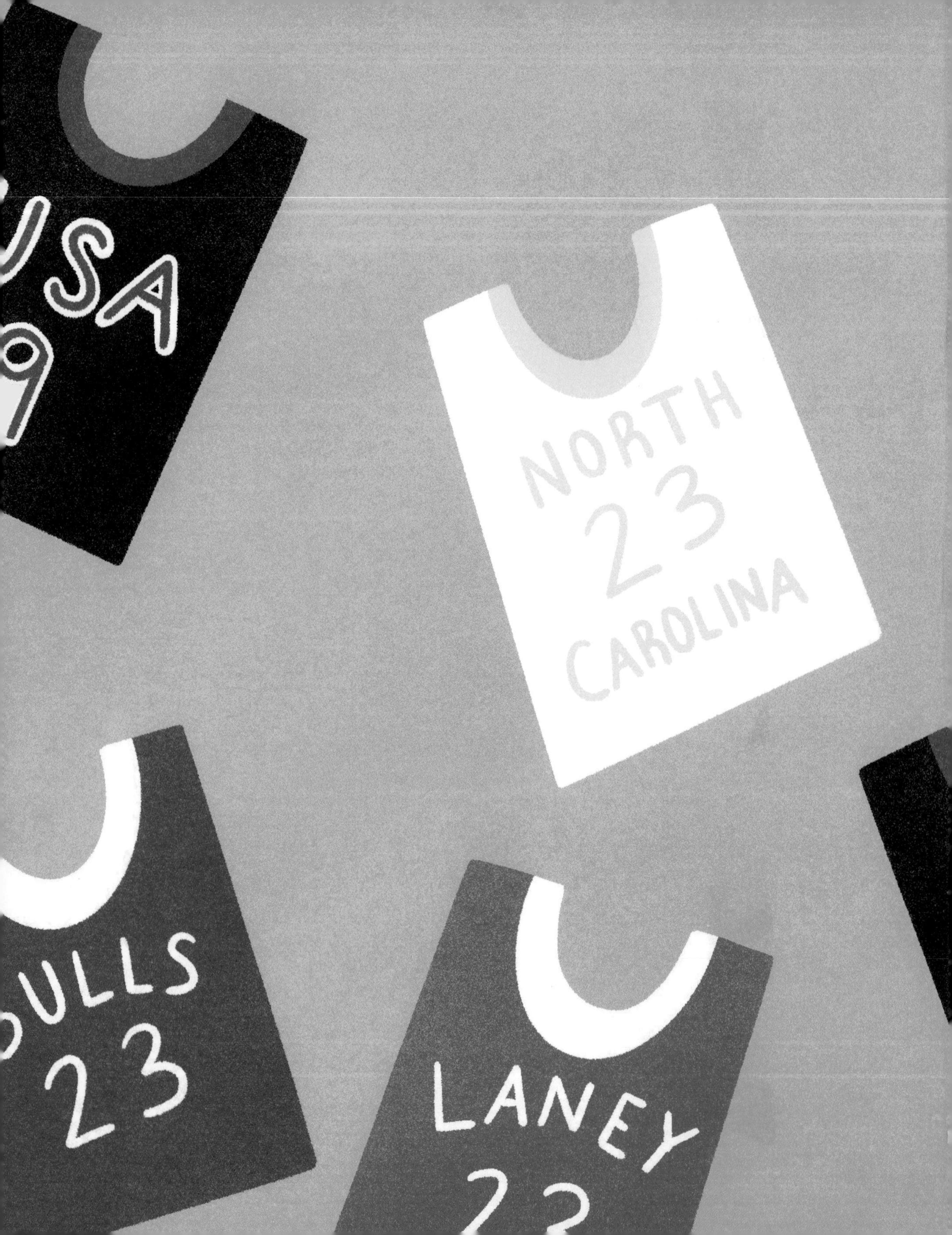
NORTH
23
CAROLINA
23
LANEY